100 QUESTIONS about the AMAZON RAINFOREST

and all
the answers
too!

Written and Illustrated by
Simon Abbott

PETER PAUPER PRESS, INC.
White Plains, New York

PETER PAUPER PRESS

In 1928, at the age of twenty-two, Peter Beilenson began printing books on a small press in the basement of his parents' home in Larchmont, New York. Peter—and later, his wife, Edna—sought to create fine books that sold at "prices even a pauper could afford."

Today, still family owned and operated, Peter Pauper Press continues to honor our founders' legacy of quality, value, and fun for big kids and small kids alike.

Designed by Heather Zschock

Text and illustrations copyright © 2020 by Simon Abbott

Published by Peter Pauper Press, Inc.
202 Mamaroneck Avenue
White Plains, New York 10601 USA

Published in the United Kingdom and Europe by Peter Pauper Press, Inc.
c/o White Pebble International
Unit 2, Plot 11 Terminus Rd.
Chichester, West Sussex PO19 8TX, UK

Library of Congress Cataloging-in-Publication Data Available

ISBN 978-1-4413-3437-4
Manufactured for Peter Pauper Press, Inc.
Printed in Hong Kong

7 6 5 4 3 2 1

Visit us at www.peterpauper.com

WELCOME

to the amazing Amazon rainforest!

Let's swing through the trees and discover all there is to know about this incredible ecosystem.

Why is the rainforest called "the lungs of the planet"?

How long would it take to swim the length of the Amazon River?

How many tribes call the rainforest home?

Lace up your walking boots to uncover the answers to these questions and more. Get ready to take a hike along the forest floor and unearth some fantastic facts!

WHERE IN THE WORLD?

Let's discover where the Amazon rainforest is. Roll out the map!

Where is this rainforest exactly?

The **Amazon basin** covers 40 percent of **South America**. This dense, tropical forest stretches over 2,100,000 square miles (5,500,000 km²), making it the largest rainforest in the world.

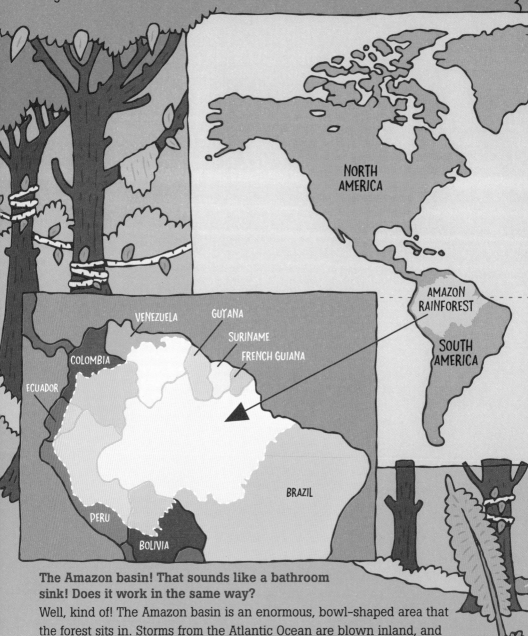

The Amazon basin! That sounds like a bathroom sink! Does it work in the same way?

Well, kind of! The Amazon basin is an enormous, bowl-shaped area that the forest sits in. Storms from the Atlantic Ocean are blown inland, and rain collects in the basin.

Does the rainforest flood?

Some of the rainwater feeds the forest, and the rest flows into the Amazon River. However, heavy seasonal rain can flood over 150,000 square miles (388,000 km²) of forest, with water levels up to 49 feet (15 m) deep. That's as tall as a five-story building!

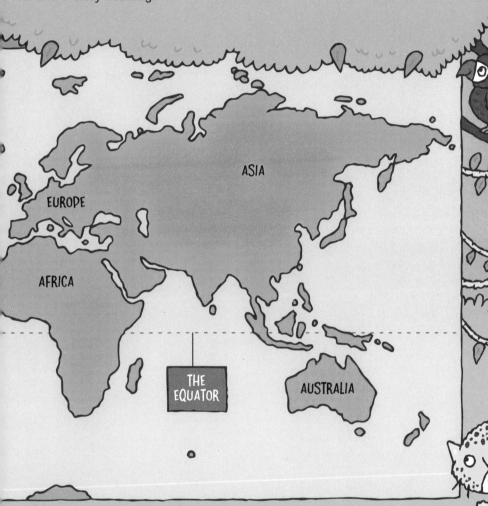

EUROPE

ASIA

AFRICA

THE EQUATOR

AUSTRALIA

Which country is the rainforest in?

The Amazon rainforest is so vast that it sprawls across eight countries on both sides of the equator. You'll find the rainforest in Bolivia, Brazil, Colombia, Ecuador, Guyana, Peru, Suriname, Venezuela, and French Guiana.

What is the equator?

This is an imaginary line running around the middle of planet Earth. Areas around the equator are called the **tropics**, so the Amazon is a **tropical** rainforest.

Are tropical rainforests found in other places on Earth?
Sure! In fact, they cover around 6 percent of Earth's surface. Tropical rainforests are dotted along the equator, from the Democratic Republic of the Congo to Australia, and from Malaysia to Bangladesh!

Apart from their position along the equator, what else do these rainforests have in common?
The weather! In the tropics, it's hot and humid all year round, with temperatures in the Amazon rainforest hitting a steamy 91°F (33°C). On average, the Amazon experiences a torrential 8 feet (2.5 m) to 10 feet (3 m) of rain every year. That's half the height of a giraffe! Heat and water create perfect conditions for dense jungles to thrive.

Does the forest's heat and moisture create fertile soil and rich crops?
Surprisingly, no! Tropical soils are often thin, with very poor mineral content.
The heavy rainfall can wash nutrients away, and the heat can decompose dead
things far too quickly. This is why slash-and-burn techniques (in which sections
of forest are burnt as they're cleared) are often used for farming: because
burnt plants release nutrients back into the soil.

**Is the Amazon rainforest just jammed with trees,
shrubs, and other plants?**
Well, there are around 390 billion trees in this diverse ecosystem,
but it's home to many humans. There are several big cities in the Amazon
rainforest, such as Iquitos in Peru, which boasts a population of 430,000 people.
Just don't expect to get there by road. Iquitos is surrounded by forest,
so its only links to the outside world are by river or by air.

TERRIFIC TREES AND PHENOMENAL PLANTS!

It's time to branch out and untangle the forest's facts.
You won't be-leaf it!

Are the trees that make up the Amazon rainforest all one type?

No! The Amazon is home to about 80,000 different plant species, including between 40 and 100 species of tree per hectare (2.5 acres, or 10,000 m^2). Around half of these are essential in controlling our planet's climate.

Why are the Amazon's plants such a vital part of life on Earth?

Plants take in carbon dioxide and release oxygen as part of the photosynthesis process they use to create food. How convenient, since animals—including people—do the exact opposite, taking in oxygen and releasing carbon dioxide when breathing. Because the Amazon rainforest provides so much of our oxygen, it's known as "the lungs of the planet."

Which plants should I try to avoid?

I would dodge Strychnos toxifera. This woody vine is a source of the poison curare, which Amazonian tribes have used to make toxic arrows. Curare is a toxic chemical that relaxes the muscles, which means if it gets in your system, it can cause muscle spasms, changes in blood pressure, and even suffocation.

Which Amazonian plants are world-record holders?

Let's hear it for the world's largest water lily, called Victoria amazonica! This super-sized specimen measures up to 10 feet (3 m) across, and is kept afloat by a system of air-filled veins. This mammoth lily pad is strong enough to support a well-balanced (and well-behaved) adult.

Economically, the rubber tree may be the most important rainforest plant. When cut, its inner bark oozes latex, which is used to make rubber tires, erasers, paint, glue, rubber boots, and many other things you use every day.

Do the rainforest's trees and plants all grow at the same speed?
Because the rainforest is so dense, the trees and plants at different heights receive different amounts of rainfall and sunlight. This means plants with different light and water requirements grow at different rates in each of the four layers of the rainforest.

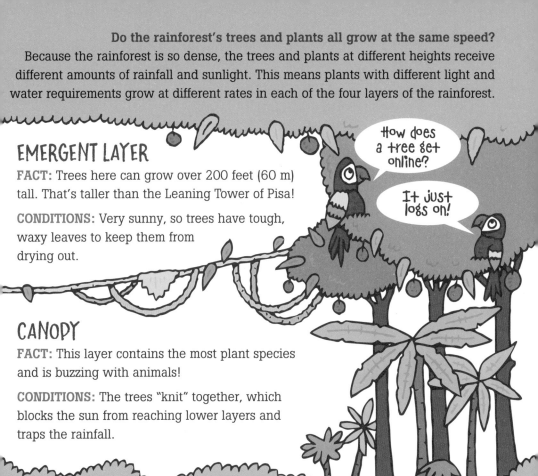

EMERGENT LAYER

FACT: Trees here can grow over 200 feet (60 m) tall. That's taller than the Leaning Tower of Pisa!

CONDITIONS: Very sunny, so trees have tough, waxy leaves to keep them from drying out.

CANOPY

FACT: This layer contains the most plant species and is buzzing with animals!

CONDITIONS: The trees "knit" together, which blocks the sun from reaching lower layers and traps the rainfall.

UNDERSTORY

FACT: Trees here rarely grow above 12 feet (3.6 m). That's about twice the length of your bed.

CONDITIONS: Warm, shaded, and damp—perfect for the large-leafed shrubs that grow there!

FOREST FLOOR

FACT:
Only 2 percent of sunlight gets through the layers above to reach the forest floor.

CONDITIONS:
Take a flashlight! It's dark, hot, and damp!

THE RAINFOREST'S RIVER

It's time to dive in and get the low-down on this record-breaking river.

Where does the Amazon River start?

The source of the river is thought to be in southern Peru, in either Nevado Mismi (a glacial mountain) or the Mantaro River. The river Apurímac may also feed the Amazon when the Mantaro is dry. The Amazon ends at the Atlantic Ocean in Brazil.

AMAZON RIVER ROUTE

AMAZON RAINFOREST

SOUTH AMERICA

Is it the longest river in the world?

Possibly! Because experts still aren't sure where the Amazon begins, we only have a rough estimate for how long it actually is. According to official counts, the Amazon River clocks in at an impressive 4,000 miles (6,400 km) long. However, the other contender, the Nile River in Africa, is 4,132 miles (6,650 km) long.

THE RIVAL—NILE RIVER!

How much water is in the Amazon?

The Amazon River carries a massive amount of water, and it empties a staggering 58 million gallons (219 million liters) into the Atlantic Ocean EVERY SECOND! It's also the widest river in the world. The mouth of the Amazon River is over 200 miles (320 km) wide.

MOUTH OF THE AMAZON

200 MILES

Has anyone been brave enough to swim along the entire river?

Drumroll for the Slovenian swimmer Martin Strel! After conquering the Danube, Mississippi, and Yangtze rivers, this incredible athlete took 67 days to complete the entire length of the Amazon. It's amazing what you can achieve when you're being chased by piranhas!

FINISH THIS WAY!

Which river creatures might Martin have spotted on his intrepid adventure?
The **Amazon manatee** may have popped its head up through the murky waters.
During historic voyages, these large aquatic mammals were sometimes mistaken
for mermaids!

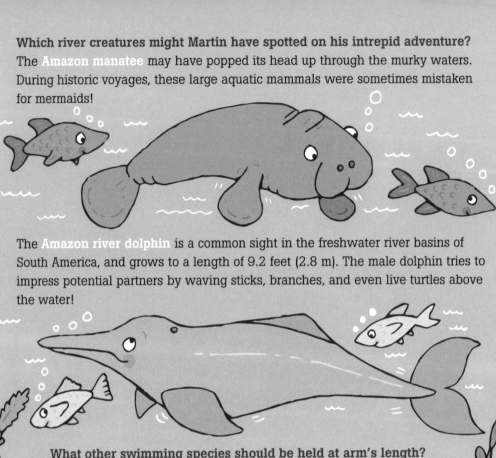

The **Amazon river dolphin** is a common sight in the freshwater river basins of
South America, and grows to a length of 9.2 feet (2.8 m). The male dolphin tries to
impress potential partners by waving sticks, branches, and even live turtles above
the water!

What other swimming species should be held at arm's length?
The **black caiman**, which looks like an alligator, can grow up to 20 feet
(6 m) long, and mostly chows down on fish, insects, and smaller mammals.
This fierce hunter will go after larger amounts and sizes of prey as it gets
older. Sometimes it will even attack people!

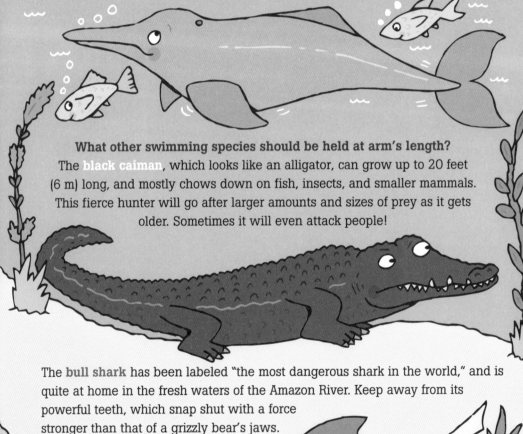

The **bull shark** has been labeled "the most dangerous shark in the world," and is
quite at home in the fresh waters of the Amazon River. Keep away from its
powerful teeth, which snap shut with a force
stronger than that of a grizzly bear's jaws.

Which Amazonian river inhabitants win the Oddball Award?
Third place goes to the **arapaima**, a massive freshwater specimen. This
10-foot (3 m) mega-fish sucks up its food like a vacuum and regularly emerges
from the river to gulp in air with a sound like a cough. This omnivorous
creature even has teeth on its tongue!

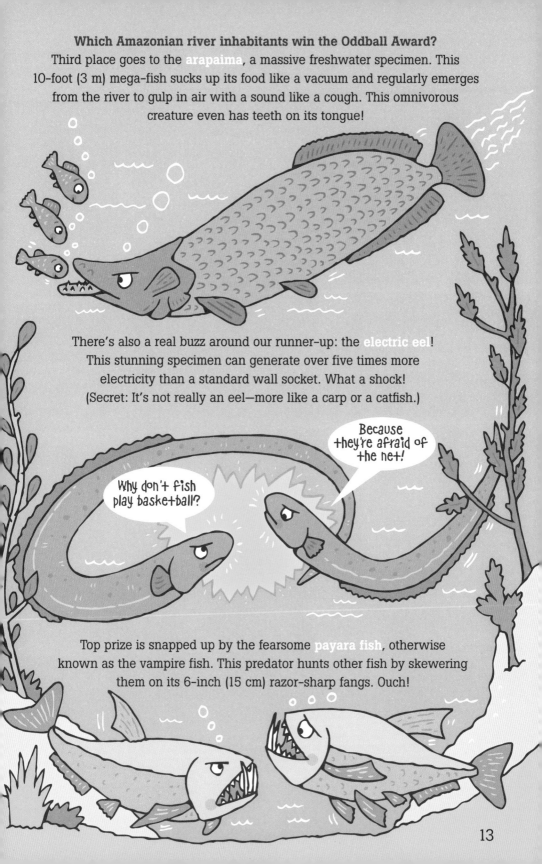

There's also a real buzz around our runner-up: the **electric eel**!
This stunning specimen can generate over five times more
electricity than a standard wall socket. What a shock!
(Secret: It's not really an eel—more like a carp or a catfish.)

Top prize is snapped up by the fearsome **payara fish**, otherwise
known as the vampire fish. This predator hunts other fish by skewering
them on its 6-inch (15 cm) razor-sharp fangs. Ouch!

AMAZING AMPHIBIANS AND REMARKABLE REPTILES

It's time to get up close with some of the Amazon's curious creatures!

First things first. What is an amphibian?

It's a group of animals, like mammals and birds. Amphibians are vertebrates (they have a backbone), are cold-blooded, and can live both in water (breathing through their skin, or sometimes through gills) and on land (breathing with their lungs). There are three main amphibian groups: frogs/toads, salamanders/newts, and worm-like caecilians.

Which group is most common in the Amazon?

There are over 400 different species of toads, frogs, and tree frogs in the rainforest. Keep away from the saucer-sized giant cane toad. Its skin gives off an irritating goop, and it can kill small predators by squirting venom from its back.

How do these slippery, smooth-skinned creatures climb through the rainforest?
Tree frogs have sticky pads on their toes. A part of these pads oozes a glue-like mucus, which helps them cling to vertical trees or the undersides of leaves.

Which other amphibians have skillfully adapted to the rainforest?
The glass frog has a translucent, or see-through, skin that reveals its internal organs. This makes it difficult for predators to spot it on its leafy perches! The female horned marsupial frog (*Gastrotheca cornuta* for short!) carries her eggs in a pouch on her back. This keeps her eggs nice and safe until the babies are ready to strike out on their own. The eggs hatch into fully-formed froglets, rather than tadpoles.

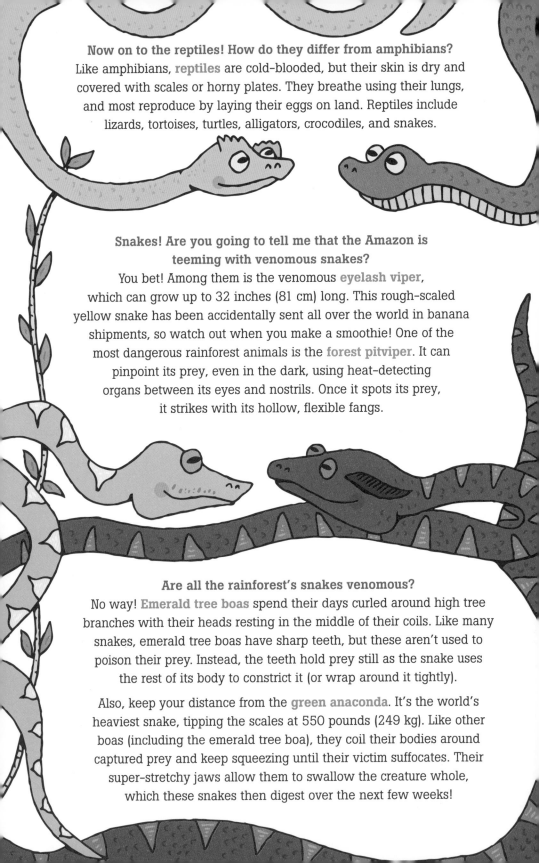

Now on to the reptiles! How do they differ from amphibians?
Like amphibians, reptiles are cold-blooded, but their skin is dry and covered with scales or horny plates. They breathe using their lungs, and most reproduce by laying their eggs on land. Reptiles include lizards, tortoises, turtles, alligators, crocodiles, and snakes.

Snakes! Are you going to tell me that the Amazon is teeming with venomous snakes?
You bet! Among them is the venomous eyelash viper, which can grow up to 32 inches (81 cm) long. This rough-scaled yellow snake has been accidentally sent all over the world in banana shipments, so watch out when you make a smoothie! One of the most dangerous rainforest animals is the forest pitviper. It can pinpoint its prey, even in the dark, using heat-detecting organs between its eyes and nostrils. Once it spots its prey, it strikes with its hollow, flexible fangs.

Are all the rainforest's snakes venomous?
No way! Emerald tree boas spend their days curled around high tree branches with their heads resting in the middle of their coils. Like many snakes, emerald tree boas have sharp teeth, but these aren't used to poison their prey. Instead, the teeth hold prey still as the snake uses the rest of its body to constrict it (or wrap around it tightly).

Also, keep your distance from the green anaconda. It's the world's heaviest snake, tipping the scales at 550 pounds (249 kg). Like other boas (including the emerald tree boa), they coil their bodies around captured prey and keep squeezing until their victim suffocates. Their super-stretchy jaws allow them to swallow the creature whole, which these snakes then digest over the next few weeks!

Which other reptiles call the Amazon home?
Let's have a glimpse at these stand-out species:

NAME: Side-necked turtle

FACT: They pull their heads and necks to the side, tucking their tender skulls underneath their protective shells, rather than retracting their heads completely inside like other turtles do.

NAME: Giant South American river turtle

FACT: When we call this turtle giant, we mean giant . . . for a turtle! The sizable female has a shell over 30 inches (76 cm) long. Before they became an endangered species, females also traveled in packs of anywhere from tens to thousands. Sadly, this habit and their size meant they were easier to poach, which is why they're endangered.

NAME: Turnip-tailed gecko

FACT: These nocturnal lizards sleep all day on tree trunks, beneath decayed logs, under bark, or on palm fronds. They have two built-in defense mechanisms: the ability to parachute (or slow the speed at which they drop) and, if caught, the ability to detach their tails!

NAME: Caiman

FACT: These super-clever creatures know how to look after their young. The females lay up to 30 eggs in a nest made of twigs, leaves, bark, and soil. As this material rots, it creates heat, which keeps the eggs warm. But check this out: Colder nest temperatures produce female hatchlings, and warmer temperatures result in males!

17

THE BUSTLING FOREST FLOOR

Grab your flashlight—we're heading to the dark and damp forest floor. Don't trip!

The forest floor is in permanent darkness due to the huge canopy of trees and leaves above it. What, besides animals, can survive in these conditions? Some young trees, called saplings, and large-leaved shrubs spring up in the small patches of sunlight left by fallen trees. Mushrooms and other fungi thrive by breaking down the decaying plant matter on the forest floor, such as rotten wood and fallen leaves. Moss and ferns are plants that continue to tough it out in these harsh conditions, usually by growing on other plants.

Which plant wins the Survive and Thrive Award?

The trophy goes to the **strangler fig tree**. Many birds, bats, and other rainforest creatures rely on figs for nutrition. Often these animals' seed-laden poop, deposited high in a tree canopy, gives rise to more strangler figs. As they grow, the seedlings' roots curl down the trunk of the host tree and dig in when they reach the ground. Over time, the strangler fig's roots will choke the host tree, and the fig's large leaves will block out the host's sunlight. Soon all that's left of the host tree will be a hollow, rotten trunk.

Which adaptable animals live in this difficult environment?

Giant anteaters tear open ant nests and mounds with their sharp claws, then use their long, sticky tongues to quickly flick up prey. You might spot a **jaguar** with its distinctive spotted coat. Unlike your pet cat, jaguars are not afraid of water and often swim in the Amazon River to hunt for fish, turtles, and caiman. The **tapir** is an ancient animal with a short, stubby trunk, which it uses to pluck fruit or strip leaves from a branch. It dives into the river to cool off, nibbles on aquatic plants, or wallows in Amazonian mud!

MARVELOUS MINI-BEASTS

Shall we wriggle along and unearth the insects that crawl and creep around the rainforest? What's the buzz on these Amazonian bugs?

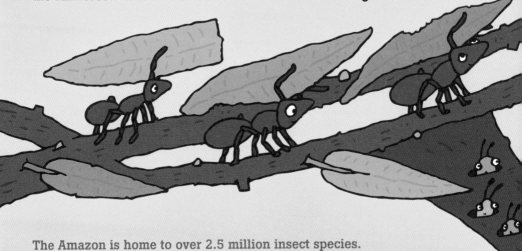

The Amazon is home to over 2.5 million insect species.
Which type is most plentiful?
Some scientists believe that **ants** make up 30 percent of the animal biomass in the Amazon basin! **Leaf cutter ants** live together in colossal colonies and build huge anthills with complex tunnel systems and multiple entrances. The **bullet ant** has an incredibly painful sting and bite combination, 30 times more painful than a bee's! As part of a ritual to enter adulthood, some young Sateré-Mawé Amazon tribesmen have to endure this sting by repeatedly putting their hands into an ant-filled glove for 10 minutes at a time.

Sounds painful! Which other aggressive ants are badly behaved?
It's not a surprise that **army ants** have a dangerous reputation! Some species form armies of half a million ants and march over the forest floor to prey on insects (including fellow ants), spiders, frogs, lizards, and birds. On a bad day, they can kill up to 30,000 animals! The **Allomerus** (a type of tree ant) goes to the trouble of building traps woven from hair-like plant fibers. These cunning ants hide underneath their traps, just waiting for an unsuspecting victim to drop by!

Which street-smart mini-beasts are cool under pressure?
The **click beetle** can get itself out of a sticky situation. If the beetle is under attack, muscles in its thorax jerk, flinging it into the air. While sailing through the air, it makes the powerful clicking noise for which it's named, which is meant to frighten off its attacker.

21

I spy a spider! What's one of our eight-legged rainforest friends?
Let's hear it for the **giant fishing spider.** This spider can grow up to 4 inches (12 cm) wide and is often found near water, waiting for the slightest ripple made by an insect or small fish. It then swims out to grab the unsuspecting victim and haul it to dry land.

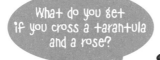

What do you get if you cross a tarantula and a rose?

I don't know, but I won't try smelling it!

I think I can figure out the diet of the
Goliath birdeater! Does it feast on anything else?
Sure! This spider actually more often enjoys snacking on insects,
but will catch the odd rodent, reptile, and (of course) bird, too.
The Goliath birdeater finds it hard to eat solid food, so it liquefies
the insides of its victims, then sucks them dry.

Which spiders should I avoid?
The above-mentioned Goliath birdeater is among the largest spiders in the world and can measure up to 12 inches (31 cm) across. That's bigger than a dinner plate! Its bite feels like a bee sting to humans, though, so it shouldn't inflict any long-term damage. However, try to avoid the **Brazilian wandering spider**. Its deadly bite can kill an adult in less than a half an hour.

Are spiders the real kings of the jungle?
Nope! The 12-inch (30 cm) long Amazonian giant centipede can kill off a Goliath birdeater with a single bite! This aggressive bug has fangs that can inject venom into frogs, rats, birds, and snakes. At 430 million years old centipedes are some of the oldest venom-carrying animals on the planet.

Which colorful creatures are the marvels of the mini-beast world?
The butterflies! The glasswing butterfly is an extra-special species with a pair of see-through wings. The Julia butterfly has beautiful yellow or orange wings and an unusual habit of drinking water from the eyes of turtles and caiman. They tear-feed to get at minerals, such as sodium, which can be hard to find in nature.

The blue morpho butterfly has a number of defensive strategies when it's under attack. The undersides of its wings are camouflaged in tones of brown, red, black, and gray, which lets it blend in with the surrounding plants. When in flight, its wings flash from the bright blue of their top sides to the dull brown underneath, making these butterflies even harder to spot in the dense jungle vegetation.

MAMMALS AND MONKEYS— OH MY!

Onward and upward! Let's look at the furry animals that call the rainforest home.

What is the curious-looking creature pictured below?
Let's meet the **giant armadillo**! These shy, nocturnal creatures dig deep burrows, but only live there for a couple of nights before moving on to a new location. Once they're gone, pumas, wild pigs, tapirs, anteaters, or turtles move in! On their travels, the nomadic giant armadillos can cover a home range of 8 square miles (20 km^2). That's about six times the size of New York's Central Park!

Wow! Are all Amazonian animals that energetic?
Hardly! The **three-toed sloth** is the slowest mammal on Earth. In fact, it's so slow that green algae can grow on its fur (which is a handy camouflage in the rainforest). A sloth's long, gripping claws allow it to hang from tree branches, where it can sleep for 15 to 20 hours a day!

The world's slowest mammal! That's some achievement!
Is the Amazon home to any other record-breakers?
The **capybara** is the world's largest rodent. These creatures look like
super-sized guinea pigs and can grow to the size of a large dog.

As its name suggests, the **giant otter** is another champion.
This animal can measure up to 6 feet (1.8 m) long and can swim at great
speeds with its powerful tail, muscular body, and webbed feet.

Which exceptional Amazonian mammal is a real one-of-a-kind?
Let's hear it for the **spectacled bear**, the only bear on the South American
continent. These small-scale solitary creatures grow to around 6 feet (1.83 m)
tall and weigh around 340 pounds (154 kg). In comparison, a grizzly bear tips
the scales at a hefty 1,700 pounds (770 kg). The spectacled bear isn't as
aggressive as a grizzly either. In fact, it's mostly vegetarian! A great climber
and extremely patient, it's been known to sit on a bed of twigs and
branches high in the trees, waiting for fruit to ripen.

25

I'd think the Amazon rainforest would be a calm, quiet, and peaceful place. Would that be true?

You've never heard the male black howler monkey, then! When a group of these creatures howl, their loud calls can be heard up to 3 miles (4.8 km) away! Their echoing, deep howls are created by the monkey's oversized throat and shell-like vocal chamber, which amplifies their yells to an ear-bashing volume!

Why do they make such a racket?

Simple: To send out the warning, "Stay away! This tree is taken!" They can also use their calls to keep track of one another.

What kind of key opens a banana?

A mon-key!

Do any other Amazonian mammals use their voices in this way?

Most animals communicate through sound in one way or another. However, a sneaky forest cat called the margay can mimic the sound of a baby pied tamarin monkey. It does this to attract the attention of adult monkeys nearby, who might be fooled into creeping closer to the jungle cat and come under attack.

**Let's branch out and take a monkey roll call.
Who will we find swinging through the tree canopy?**

Night Monkey (aka Owl Monkey)
Their large brown eyes help them see in the dark.

Red Titi Monkey (pronounced *tee-TEE*)
These romantic mammals mate for life and
sleep in pairs with their tails entwined.

Pygmy Marmoset
The pygmy marmoset is the smallest
monkey in the world. This tiny monkey
weighs 3.5 ounces (99 g)—just a little
more than a deck of cards! Not only that,
but at 6 inches (15 cm) tall, it's also less
than two-thirds the height of this book!

Spider Monkey
These agile animals use their long tails to grip
tree branches like an extra arm or hand.

Capuchin Monkey
These super-clever creatures have been known to
use simple tools to hammer, dig, and pound nuts.

FANTASTIC FLYERS

It's time to flutter through the forest and search out our feathered friends.

It's no surprise to find that the rainforest is home to some unbelievable birds. How many different species would you come across?

There are over 1,300 species of birds in the Amazon rainforest. Some are unique to the region, and other birds **migrate** from North America between November and March.

What does migrate mean?

Every year, some birds (and other animals) leave their summer habitats to spend the winter months in warmer environments where they can feed and reproduce. The **upland sandpiper**, for instance, travels 6,000 miles (9,656 km) from its home in the grasslands of North America to the South American rainforests, taking a route called the **Central Flyway**, a path many migratory birds use down the center of North America. Then they return north for the summer.

CENTRAL
FLYWAY

Which Amazonian bird is the most well-known?

I would put money on the scarlet macaw, the mostly red, hook-beaked bird you probably think of when you hear the word "parrot." This bird has brightly colored feathers, a powerful beak to crack open nuts and seeds, and a hard, scaly tongue. Its beak and tongue are ideal for piercing juicy fruits!

Are all Amazonian birds herbivores?

As you may know, an **herbivore** eats only plants, a **carnivore** eats meat, and an animal that eats both is called an **omnivore**. But back to the question. The rainforest is home to birds with all three diet varieties. The carnivorous **harpy eagle** is known as an **apex predator**. This means it's right at the top of the food chain, with no known natural predators. It hunts sloths, monkeys, and opossums, with the occasional iguana and macaw to mix it up a little. The colorful **toucan** is a fine example of an omnivore. They use their jagged-edged 7.5-inch (19-cm) bills to peel fruit and snack on insects, eggs, and newly-hatched birds.

Before we fly away, which stand-out facts do I need to know about the birds of the Amazon rainforest?

Hummingbirds are definitely worth a mention. There are over 300 species of hummingbird in the Amazon alone! Did you know that hummingbirds are the only birds in the world that can fly both forward and backward? Not only that, but they can hover in mid-air, fly sideways, and even zoom along upside down!

Some feathered friends have a real sweet tooth! Which birds get territorial as they protect their sugar supplies?

The vibrant crimson topaz hummingbird defends its feeding patch of highly sugary flowers aggressively. Males will chase away rivals to their sweet treats (such as bumblebees and moths) with chattering calls and threatening displays. Both male and female crimson topaz hummingbirds will hover around flowers and use their extendable tongues to lick at the nectar up to 13 times per second. Talk about a sugar rush!

HOME SWEET HOME!

Let's introduce ourselves to the people who live, grow, work, and celebrate in the Amazon Rainforest.

How long have humans been living in the Amazon rainforest?

About 13,000 years! Before the arrival of European explorers in the 16th century, millions of native people already lived in South America—many in the Amazon rainforest.

Did these native people live together in one vast city?

These indigenous (*in-DIH-jen-us*—that means native) people grouped together in tribes, including the **Yanomami** and **Palikur** tribes. There are still around 400 tribes that inhabit the rainforest today, with an incredible 300 languages being spoken among them.

How did the ancient tribes survive?

Most tribes settled along or close to the river, where there's access to fresh water. There is evidence that these tribes have been farming plants native to the surrounding forest for around 8,000 years. Small patches of land would be cleared, and crops (including corn, sweet potato, cacao, brazil nuts, and squash) would be planted, with fruits such as the **açaí berry** adding to their diet. Tribes close to the Amazon River would hunt for fish, turtles, capybara, and crocodiles with blow-guns, poison darts, bows, and arrows. A few tribes were also nomadic (meaning they moved around a lot) and relied more on hunting than farming or fishing.

Native Amazonians from many cultures depended on their tribe's shaman, who collected invaluable knowledge about ailments and diseases from previous generations. The rainforest is brimming with natural plant cures. Take a glimpse at the Amazon medicine cabinet:

Cinchona Tree

Ground-up bark from this tree was one of the first treatments for **malaria**, a deadly disease carried by the tropical mosquitoes that infest the rainforest. This bark is also handy for treating muscle spasms and chills!

THE SHAMAN IS **IN**

Cordoncillo

A natural **anesthetic** (*an-ehs-TEHT-ic*). Chew the leaves, and your mouth will go numb!

Sangre de Grado

Natives used sap from this plant to stop bleeding, but it's used in modern medicine to treat a wide variety of ailments, from ulcers to infections.

Shapumvilla

It can also be used to stop bleeding. (Very handy if you have an accident with a blow gun!)

Where do modern-day Amazonian tribes live? What are their homes like?
Building styles vary from culture to culture. In the **Yanomami** society, they
construct large, circular houses called **yamos** or **shabonos** from leaves, vines,
and tree trunks. Some are large enough for 400 people! Each family has their
own fire for cooking and for staying warm through the night as they sleep in
their hammocks.

What did the nut say when it sneezed?

Cashew!

Does the Yanomami society have a single leader?
No. Equality among all people is the key to this tribe's success.
Everyone has a say, and decisions are made after long debates.
A hunter will share the meat he catches, rather than eat it himself,
but in return, other hunters will give him portions of their meat.
Women play a vital role in growing crops, collecting nuts and
shellfish, and making the sought-after wild honey.

How do the Yanomami have fun?

A good harvest is celebrated with a huge feast. The whole village is invited, and they decorate their bodies with feathers and flowers. The Yanomami sing traditional songs about the tribe's history and dance into the night. These songs are sometimes accompanied by flutes made from bamboo or animal bones. Sounds like fun!

Are all Amazonian tribes organized like the Yanomami?

Outsiders don't know! Some isolated rainforest societies have no connection to the outside world. There are an estimated 80 **uncontacted** tribes living in the Brazilian Amazon alone, which is hard to believe in a world buzzing with smart phones, social media, and the internet.

EXCITING EXPLORATIONS!

Who were the first European adventurers to explore the Amazon rainforest? Let's see what they made of this extraordinary ecosystem.

Why did the European explorers make the treacherous journey to South America?

The Spanish adventurer **Francisco de Orellana** was on a mission to discover the legendary (but fictitious) **El Dorado**, supposedly a city full of gold. His expedition didn't go well, and he was forced to take a boat down the Rio Napo in search of fresh supplies. Despite numerous skirmishes with tribes along the route (who were probably pretty surprised and alarmed to see him), de Orellana navigated the Amazon River and finally reached the Atlantic Ocean in August, 1542.

What did de Orellana do as soon as he made it?

De Orellana returned home and bragged to the Spanish king about his victories over the strong and fearless tribesmen and women. He compared them to Amazon warriors in stories from ancient Greece, which is how the rainforest and river got their European name.

Did other explorers line up to make the trip?

Not surprisingly, there wasn't much interest in voyaging to a dense, steamy forest full of inhospitable locals. One exception was **Francisco Pizarro**, who journeyed through the Amazon in the 16th century . . . and brutally conquered the Inca Empire to steal an enormous hoard of treasure.

It sounds like these Europeans were a dreadful mob. Were there any visitors to the Amazon who were a force for good?

The German naturalist **Alexander von Humboldt** traveled to the Amazon in 1799, and spent five years covering 6,000 miles (9,650 km) on horseback, on foot, and in canoes. He climbed mountains, descended into mines, and survived encounters with alligators, giant spiders, and jaguars. What he saw in the rainforest helped him understand man's effect on the environment, and he became the first scientist to consider **climate change**. He concluded that trees, soil, climate, and life were all connected.

Fifty years later, in 1848, the British naturalist **Henry Walter Bates** arrived in Brazil at the mouth of the Amazon River. He spent the next 11 years exploring the entire Amazon basin, collecting an incredible 14,712 different species, 8,000 of which had previously been unknown to the Europeans! He was helped on his mission by the native Amazon tribespeople, and in turn, he learned many native languages and customs.

Which invention was bad news for the Amazon?

Vulcanized rubber. Although local tribes had been using the sap from rubber trees for hundreds of years, French scientist **Charles de la Condamine** claimed to have discovered it in 1735 while in Peru. He brought it back to Europe, but it took years for someone to find something handy to do with it. In 1844, **Charles Goodyear** patented a process called **vulcanization**, which made rubber waterproof and winter-proof. Perfect for tires! When inflatable tires were sold worldwide in the 1890s, the demand for rubber exploded. Plantations sprang up throughout the Amazon, and indigenous tribes were enslaved and forced to work in brutal conditions.

What European import had an even more catastrophic effect on the rainforest?

Unknowingly, European explorers brought with them smallpox, measles, and even the common cold. The indigenous people had no resistance to these diseases, as they had never been exposed to such illnesses before. Epidemics decimated the local population, and over 90 percent of native people died as the diseases spread.

A NATURAL RESOURCE

The seven billion people on Earth need one thing: food! How does farming in the Amazon rainforest help to satisfy this demand?

Farming in a rainforest! Are you sure?
In Brazil alone, 93 million acres of the Amazon are used for agriculture. That's about the size of the U.S. state of Montana!

What produce is grown in the rainforest?
The crops most suited to the poor Amazon soil are **rice**, **soybeans**, **bananas**, **citrus**, **palm oil**, **coffee**, and **cacao**. These are known as **cash crops**, which are sold to make money for the landowners.

Are any of these crops farmed more than others?
Soy is a key part of the Earth's food supply. It's used mainly in animal feed, so as the global demand for meat products increases, so does the demand for more soy. China alone imported around 88 million tons of soybeans in 2019, just to give you an idea of how much demand there is for these little beans.

**Do the Amazonian crops grow easily underneath
the dense rainforest tree canopy?**

No. Forest clearers must use a technique called **slash and burn**,
which is when farmers burn plants to release nutrients back into
unfertile soil. Fires from this forest-clearing spree can be huge.
Moreover, once the nutrients in the soil are used up again, the land is
abandoned, and farmers move on to clear a new area of rainforest.

What other types of farms would I see if I visited the rainforest?

The global demand for meat has meant that cattle farms have aggressively
expanded through huge areas of the Amazon. **Cattle ranching** accounts for around
80 percent of deforestation, with around 174,000 square miles (450,000 square km)
now given over to cattle pasture. That's a bigger piece of land than California! As of
this writing, Brazil produces over 9 million metric tons of beef every year (1 million
tons of which leave Brazil), which means large swaths of rainforest will need to be
cleared and kept clear to raise the cattle to meet these meaty demands.

What other profitable export does the Amazon supply?
Simple—it's wood! Tropical trees are used in everything from ships to furniture, to chopsticks, to toilet seats. Mahogany, walnut, and rosewood trees are all chopped down and sold by forest loggers. Of these, mahogany, with its hardness and rich color, is in the highest demand.

Is rubber still an important rainforest resource?
Today, 90 percent of the world's natural rubber supply comes from Southeast Asia, now that the Amazon rubber boom of 1879 to 1912 is long over. However, wild rubber still provides a vital income for families making a living in remote parts of the forest.

Are any other valuable resources found in the forest?
Minerals such as **copper**, **tin**, **nickel**, **bauxite** (used to make aluminum),
manganese (used to make steel), **iron**, and **gold** are all vital resources found
beneath the rainforest soil. Huge reserves of **oil** and **natural gas**
have also been discovered under the Amazon.

Which rainforest resource would we find it hard to live without?
Medicine! Around 25 percent of all drugs used today come from a
rainforest plant. **Lapacho** tree bark is used to treat inflammation,
curare is used to treat multiple sclerosis and Parkinson's disease,
and **quinine** is an effective anti-malarial drug.

THE FRAGILE FOREST

The rainforest's resources fuel the whole world's economy. But what price does the Amazon pay to supply the increasing global demand?

Do we need to be worried about the deforestation of the Amazon?
Rainforests that once covered over 14 percent of the Earth now make up just 6 percent. In the Amazon, if the current deforestation rates continue, 27 percent (over a quarter!) of the rainforest will be without trees by 2030.

I don't live in the Amazon rainforest! How does this affect me?
The Amazon rainforest produces resources we need to live, including the air that we breathe. The large leaves of the forest's billions of trees absorb huge amounts of carbon dioxide, then release oxygen.

The Amazon is also key in the fight against climate change. Carbon dioxide (the stuff trees absorb) is what's known as a greenhouse gas: If a whole lot of it ends up in the atmosphere, it can create a blanket that warms the planet. This can result in devastating storms and the extinction of hundreds of species. As huge areas of the Amazon are burnt to clear land, carbon is released into the atmosphere, and there may be a point at which the trees are no longer able to soak up and store enough carbon.

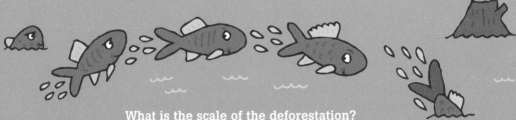

What is the scale of the deforestation?
Tens of thousands of fires are burning across the Brazilian rainforest at any one time, often covering an area the size of the U.S. state of New Jersey. Surprisingly, government rules meant to manage the clearing of forest for crops, cattle, and lumber in parts of the Amazon have loosened over recent years, allowing more of the forest to be cleared.

Deforestation devastates the rainforest—and the planet itself. How else is the Amazon being damaged?

Mining has a huge impact, because it adds to deforestation and because mined minerals can mix with water and run into the rainforest's waterways and soil with deadly results. For example, mercury, which is highly toxic, is used to help mine gold, then dumped or washed off into the surrounding water supply, where it can poison the local fish—not to mention the people who eat those fish.

Brazil has a population of 200 million people, with a huge demand for electricity. How does this affect the rainforest?

Almost 70 percent of Latin America relies on hydropower for its electricity. This cheap and plentiful energy supply uses rotating machines to convert falling water into electrical power. Rivers in the Amazon are dammed to create huge reservoirs, some as big as the U.S. state of Rhode Island. These dams can block the flow of nutrients, dry out wetland habitats, and prevent migrating fish from swimming upstream. Over time, some fish species could become extinct because dams block them from getting to their breeding grounds.

Extinct! That sounds alarming. What does it mean?
When a species goes extinct, it no longer exists—or, in other words, it's died out. So, yes, it's very alarming!

Are any other animals in danger of going extinct?
Deforestation has forced wildlife to inhabit smaller patches of the rainforest. The competition for food increases and birth rates drop. 265 endangered species of plants and animals are in danger of extinction due to the rainforest fires. Of these, 124 can only be found in the Amazon basin.

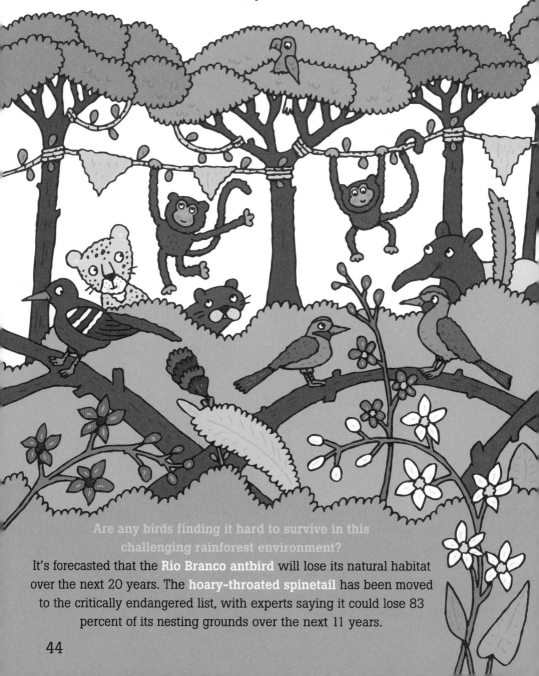

Are any birds finding it hard to survive in this challenging rainforest environment?
It's forecasted that the Rio Branco antbird will lose its natural habitat over the next 20 years. The hoary-throated spinetail has been moved to the critically endangered list, with experts saying it could lose 83 percent of its nesting grounds over the next 11 years.

Plants are, well, rooted in the Amazon **ecosystem**, so if the ecosystem is disturbed, plants become endangered. For example, the **orchid**, of which there are over 25,000 species in South America, is intertwined with the ecosystem of the Amazon. Many orchids grow in the branches of the Amazonian trees, others rely on specific animals to reproduce, and some can only grow if fungi thrive on their seeds. However, as the forest disappears, the orchids lose the trees, animals, and fungi they rely on to grow.

45

PROTECT OUR PLANET!

Are people taking action to help conserve the rainforest for future generations? The health of the planet depends on it!

What projects are underway that put a brake on the relentless deforestation?

Many organizations work tirelessly with indigenous Amazon communities to preserve the rainforest. In 2002, the **ARPA** (Amazon Region Protected Areas) was launched in Brazil. Its aim was to take 150 million acres (61 million hectares) of the rainforest and turn it into a mix of protected areas and controlled sustainable use.

How can we plant replacement trees quickly?

73 million new trees are planned in what may be the largest tropical reforestation project in history. The idea is to replant enough trees to fill 70,000 acres (28,328 hectares) of land that was cleared for cattle grazing. In fact, this initiative will use the **muvuca method**, in which a mix of seeds from 200 native species will be scattered over every 3 ft^2 (1 m^2) of barren land. It is hoped that this method will provide 6,000 to 12,000 trees per acre (0.4 hectare).

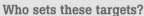

Who sets these targets?

In December 2015, nearly 200 countries got together to discuss how to tackle climate change. Countries promised to take steps to limit how much carbon they produced. Brazil, for example, agreed to reforest roughly 46,300 square miles (119,916 km^2) and to cut 43 percent of its carbon emissions by 2030. Unfortunately, the recent rainforest fires and weaker deforestation controls mean that these targets may be missed.

Why have the indigenous tribes allowed logging, mining, cattle grazing, and oil pumping on their land?

They haven't! Despite living in the Amazon rainforest for thousands of years, the land rights granted to them by Amazonian countries' constitutions are often ignored. These rights are supposed to either grant tribes legal ownership over their land or force developers and governments to consult them before every project. Instead, some governments go over the heads of tribes to let developers in anyway. However, tribes are fighting back in courts to make their voices heard and to protect their forest.

What is green and has leaves and a trunk?

A tree going on vacation!

What else is going on to help the forest?

While reforestation will bring back natural habitats for animals to live in, endangered species have been getting added help through **nature reserves** (places that are protected from poaching or development) and **breeding programs** (programs that help animals to breed safely so they and their offspring can be put back in the wild). For example, the **golden lion tamarin**, a monkey, went from about 200 animals in the wild to over 2,500 thanks to a combination of breeding programs and relocation to nature reserves such as the **Poço das Antas**.

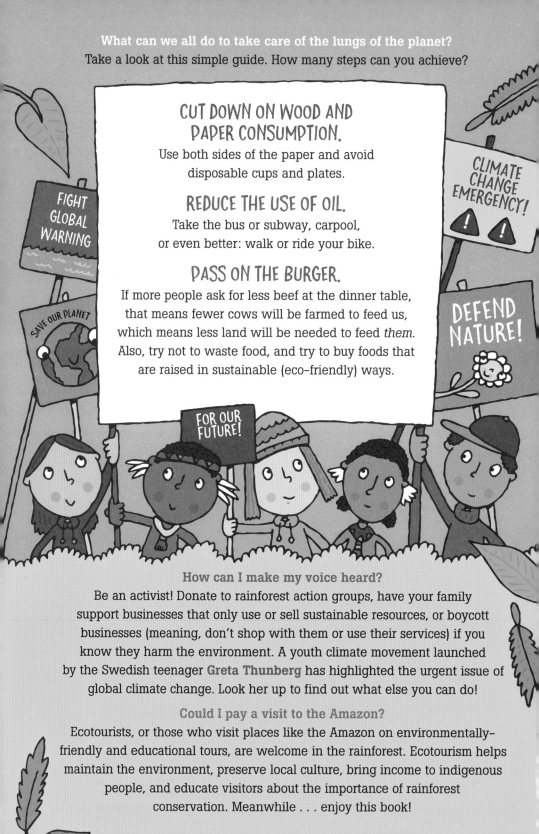

What can we all do to take care of the lungs of the planet?
Take a look at this simple guide. How many steps can you achieve?

CUT DOWN ON WOOD AND PAPER CONSUMPTION.
Use both sides of the paper and avoid
disposable cups and plates.

REDUCE THE USE OF OIL.
Take the bus or subway, carpool,
or even better: walk or ride your bike.

PASS ON THE BURGER.
If more people ask for less beef at the dinner table,
that means fewer cows will be farmed to feed us,
which means less land will be needed to feed *them*.
Also, try not to waste food, and try to buy foods that
are raised in sustainable (eco-friendly) ways.

FIGHT GLOBAL WARNING

SAVE OUR PLANET

CLIMATE CHANGE EMERGENCY!

DEFEND NATURE!

FOR OUR FUTURE!

How can I make my voice heard?
Be an activist! Donate to rainforest action groups, have your family
support businesses that only use or sell sustainable resources, or boycott
businesses (meaning, don't shop with them or use their services) if you
know they harm the environment. A youth climate movement launched
by the Swedish teenager **Greta Thunberg** has highlighted the urgent issue of
global climate change. Look her up to find out what else you can do!

Could I pay a visit to the Amazon?
Ecotourists, or those who visit places like the Amazon on environmentally-
friendly and educational tours, are welcome in the rainforest. Ecotourism helps
maintain the environment, preserve local culture, bring income to indigenous
people, and educate visitors about the importance of rainforest
conservation. Meanwhile . . . enjoy this book!